Reaching While Teaching

An Educator's Guide to Impacting and
Transforming Lives

Filled with Inspirational Stories, Daily
Prayers and Practical Advice.

Reaching While Teaching By: Shanine Alessia Young

NLT

Scripture quotations marked NLT are taken from the New Living Translation Version.

Printed in the United States of America.

ISBN: 9798643282457

Imprint: Independently published

Books may be purchased in bulk quantity and or special sales by contacting the author at
shaninealessia@gmail.com

Logo Designed by **Jordan Young**

Book Cover Designed by **T. Harty Designs, Florida**

Photography by **Eric Jackson (SoFlo Inspire)**

Dedication

I dedicate this book to my amazing and supportive husband Jordan, without his support this would not be possible, as well as my beautiful baby girl Shanel, who inspires me to be great.

I also dedicate this book to all the teachers who are trying their best to make a positive impact in the lives of their students. You are appreciated.

Acknowledgments

I would like to first thank Jesus for giving me the inspiration and revelation needed for this book.

I would like to thank my amazing editor and mother, Sherine Isom, for all the countless hours she put in to ensure I clearly expressed my thoughts in every chapter of this book.

I would like to thank my #1 Supporter, my husband Jordan Young, for all the encouraging words he has showered me with throughout the process of writing this book.

I would like to thank my dad, Terrence Isom, for instilling godly principles in me and ensuring that he raised me to be a powerful woman of God.

I would like to thank my Pastors Oral and Sandra Walters for being the most loving and sincere pastors.

I would like to thank all my friends and family who are always supporting me, my sisters, cousins, aunts, uncles, my brother, and my mother-in-love.

Special thanks to Gene Mosley for his publishing assistance and Tameka for designing my cover.

And finally, I would like to thank all my students, without you all I would not have any experiences to share.

Preface

<u>Who Are YOU?</u>

I would like to start off by telling you that YOU are special. YOU are loved by the God who created the entire universe, YOU are God's most prized possession, made in His image and created in His likeness! You are Absolutely Amazing!

YOU matter, YOU are important to God and YOU… Yes, YOU were created for a specific purpose only YOU can fulfill. There is no one with your DNA. There is no one that has all the skills and talents that God has equipped YOU with.

Whether YOU are teaching in the field of education temporarily or it is a lifelong commitment, YOU were strategically placed there by God for a reason, and there is work for YOU to do.

In the book of Psalms chapter 139 verse 16, the psalmist David says *"You saw me before I was born. Every day of my life was recorded in your book. Every moment was laid out before a single day had passed." NLT*

It is remarkable that God knew YOU before YOU even knew yourself or before your parents even knew YOU. Your appearance into this world was not a surprise to Him. He knows everything about YOU and every decision YOU will ever make or have ever made. All the days of your life are already recorded in His book, and that includes your profession.

Why Does ALL This Matter?

Why should you care about what I have to say? Why should you even keep reading? What is so important about reaching and impacting lives?

First things first, if you are a Christian, then everything in this book matters. You are called to be a light and to shine brightly in this world.

Matthew 5:14-16 are very popular verses that state:

"You are the light of the world- like a city on a hilltop that cannot be hidden. No one lights a lamp and then puts it under a basket. Instead a lamp is placed on a stand, where it gives light to everyone in the house. In the same way, Let your good deeds (light) shine out for all to see, so that everyone will praise your heavenly father." NLT

Blending is quite a common practice especially amongst the health enthusiasts. Different fruits and greens are typically blended in order to create a healthy smoothie. But no matter how popular blending gets, when it comes to your faith, you are not expected to blend. You were not called, nor were you created to simply blend in with others at work. God expects you to stand out and be unique so you can shine brightly for Him. Doing so will allow you to impact the lives of others.

I am excited to see all the lives you will impact and transform by consistently applying the principles mentioned in this book. Greatness lives within YOU, and I know you are a powerful educator that genuinely cares about your students.

Table of Contents

Mission in Writing

In her book, Shanine Alessia Young focuses on providing educators, who may or may not work in a traditional Religious School/University or any religious educational setting, with the truth they need to be powerful representatives for Christ. Young provides readers with beneficial tips and advice as well as stories and daily prayers in each chapter that will open the eyes of teachers who are truly passionate about living a life that will positively impact others. *Reaching While Teaching* is a book that not only motivates educators but gives them practical ways to reach people and overcome common educational struggles while living out their faith in and out of the classroom.

Teaching is one of the most overlooked yet powerful professions in the world. Teachers possess the ability to transform and shape minds.

This guide shows educators how to reach and teach students from different educational and socio-economic backgrounds and provides educators with practical ways to be a light at their school/educational setting. Thus, leading to impacting and transforming lives.

Do you identify with any of these titles below?

Preschool Teacher

Elementary School Teacher

Middle School Teacher

High School Teacher

Sunday School Teacher

Special Education Teacher

Homeschool Teacher

College Professor

English Language Learner Teacher

Daycare Teacher/Instructor

Tutor in any subject or field

So, if you want to be a teacher who makes a difference in the lives of those around you, then you might not want to pass up this powerful read.

Sincerely,

Shanine Alessia Young

"The mediocre teacher tells. The good teacher explains. The superior teacher demonstrates. The great teacher inspires."

-William Arthur Ward

CHAPTER 1

IT'S ALL ABOUT THE STUDENTS

Do you remember a time when you were inspired to do something? Do you remember the source of your inspiration? As an educator, you must know the importance of inspiration. Every student needs to be inspired by their teacher. Whether you are a public school, private school, homeschool, or even a Sunday School teacher, this applies to you.

According to Oxford Dictionaries, the verb *inspire* means to fill (someone) with the urge or ability to do or feel something, especially to do something creative. As educators, we should stimulate our students to learn and to think creatively. Our approach should not be mundane, where we do not stir any excitement or creativity within them.

One of my favorite quotes by William Arthur Ward helps me to keep this in perspective.

"The mediocre teacher tells. The good teacher explains. The superior teacher demonstrates. The great teacher inspires."

A Genuine Bond with your students is necessary if you really want to inspire them.

"People don't care about how much you know until they know how much you care." – Teddy Roosevelt

The love of God really needs to be evident in the way you speak to your students, the way you treat them and the way you handle situations. You are the example in the classroom, and they are most likely looking to you for guidance. When your students feel they can trust you and you genuinely care about them, they will start to open up to you more. When your students feel important, they will begin to put some more effort into their work. You will inspire them to find different ways to work that problem out. You will inspire them to write from another perspective for that essay. You will encourage them to participate more during activities.

- **Find out their likes and dislikes**: Have casual conversations with your students during any down time in class. Ask them for their opinion on your lesson or on a topic. You can even take surveys and figure out how they prefer to learn new topics. Find out some of their hobbies and if they have any talents or skills. Get to know them and what they are all about.

- **Give them plenty compliments:** Try not to be the teacher who always tells them what they are doing wrong. Tell your students what they are good at. Give them thoughtful praises for their effort, behavior, and even their attitude. Give genuine compliments, try to pick out things that most people would not notice. Your students will feel appreciated because everyone likes a nice compliment.

- **Admit when you are wrong:** When teachers lack humility, it's hard for some students to form a bond with them. Students value authenticity, and they need you to be as real and as honest as possible. If you made a mistake or you taught a previous concept incorrectly, do not be afraid to admit it. Admitting to your students when you are wrong shows them that you do not think you are better than them but that you make mistakes just like them. Owning up to your mistakes takes humility and shows them that you expect the same from them.

These are all practical things you can do that will help you form a genuine bond with your students.

Sometimes you may have to deal with difficult students.

It's easy to inspire and build bonds with students who are polite and are eager to learn, but what about those who are the complete opposite? You know… that student who always asks, "Why do we have to do this work?" and complains about every assignment. Or what about that student who thinks being disrespectful is cool? Yes… that student may not always keep you smiling but they need love and inspiration just as much as everyone else.

- **Love the Unlovable:** I had a student, let's call her Student X, who answered a question incorrectly, so I instructed her to read the section one more time since the correct answer was located there. Student X told me that she was right, that she was not going to read it again, and that I did not know what I was talking about. At that moment, I paused and said a quick prayer. I said to myself "Lord give me strength" and then I continued with the lesson. Later, I pulled her to the side, and showed her where the correct answer was located and explained why it was correct. After class, Student X came up to me and apologized for her rude comment; she went on to tell me about the problems she had been dealing with at home. The moment allowed us to bond and build a greater relationship. Had I done what my human nature/instinct wanted me to do and snapped back with a quick response showing her why she was wrong, and I was right, we would not have had the opportunity to bond. As Christian educators, we ought to have a completely different approach. If you want to be a light and inspire your students, there are times when you will have to love them even when they are unlovable. Christians are to follow Christ's example and refuse to repay evil for evil. We must love our enemies and pray for those who persecute us. (Refer to Matthew 5:44)

- **Forgive your students:** It's easier said than done but you must be quick to forgive your students. Try not to hold grudges against them. If an incident happened last week where they disrespected you, when they return to your class the following week, you should try your best to refrain from showing any hostility towards them. Love them despite their actions; after all, Christ did the same for us. (Refer to Romans 5:8) It is hard for your students to receive anything from you if they feel you are out to get them, or you don't care about them. You may not be aware of some of the challenges that your students might be dealing with. Some students struggle with living in poverty, homelessness, child abuse and neglect, violence, and even drug abuse. Some may try to mask their pain, but it comes out in different ways, such as anger, disrespect, defiance, and even laziness. These students need to feel loved when they walk into your classroom. Let your classroom or learning center be their safe place. As you show them love and be the bigger person, they can be inspired by you in many ways.

Prayer for the Day: Inspiration

Dear Heavenly Father,

Thank you for this day; thank you for this opportunity to have such a rewarding job where I can touch so many lives. Today, I ask you for peace in exchange for worry and faith in exchange for doubt. Help me not to bring any of the issues that I might be dealing with into the classroom. I pray that my students will come into the classroom ready to learn, and they will not bring any of their negativity into our learning space. I pray for wisdom when dealing with difficult situations. Let my thoughts be pure, true, and good. Lord, help me inspire my students to dream, create, and believe in themselves. I pray that this classroom will be a breeding ground for outstanding artists, doctors, scientists, authors, directors, teachers, elected officials, managers, nurses, and many more professions. I pray for more of your unconditional love and strength when I am feeling weak or feeling burned out. I ask for your guidance that I may do all that you require of me and that I will be a positive example and a godly role model for my students. Thank you in advance for allowing me to inspire my students.

Amen.

Notes

"The best thing about being a teacher is that it matters. The hardest part about being a teacher is that it matters every day."

-Todd Whitaker

CHAPTER 2

EVERY DAY COUNTS

"The best thing about being a teacher is that it matters. The hardest part about being a teacher is that it matters every day."- Todd Whitaker

I find this quote to be filled with so much truth because every day you go to work, you are entrusted with a child's or a young adult's future. You are expected to provide them with engaging lessons and lead them in the right direction every single day. Every day you play a role in shaping their mind.

You are not a robot, you are a human being with feelings and emotions, thus it is evident there will be days when you feel like your job is not important and what you are doing does not matter. However, I am here to tell you that it does. It is all about your mindset, once you realize your job is an act of service to God and to the students you teach, you will need to keep that at the forefront of your mind whenever apathy, anger or doubt tries to seep in.

What is the big deal?

Why does every day count? Why should every day matter? What is the worst that could possibly happen if you slack off every now and then? I am sure some of you might have asked yourself these questions at least once (I know I have). These are

questions that need to be addressed. I feel as though it would be a disservice to you if I just express my thoughts and provide you with helpful advice but neglect to explain my reasoning behind all of this.

So, what is the big deal? The big deal is, when you do not treat every day like it matters then you will not have a lasting impact on your students. You will allow bad habits to creep in and stay longer than you intended. You will not be able to reach out and touch the lives around you because that lackadaisical spirit will be contagious. When you slack off at your job and barely teach with any enthusiasm or excitement because "today is not your day", guess who is affected? That same spirit somehow creeps up on your students and now they are putting in less effort when completing assignments or they are refusing to even complete them. God is not pleased on those days when you slack off at your job and as you can see it brings forth negative results.

Am I saying your lessons must be perfect every single day? Am I saying you cannot make any mistakes while doing your job or the world is going to end? NO. That is far from what I am saying. What I am saying is, every day there needs to be a consistent effort that you put in despite your feelings. Every day you should value your position as an educator and think about the influence you have. Every day you are given a new opportunity to strive to be better than the day before. If you are a believer and you are reading this, then you might want to remind yourself that your job is an act of service to the Lord. You are called to work wholeheartedly as if you are working for Him and not for people.

Colossians 3:23 states ***"Work willingly at whatever you do, as though you were working for the Lord rather than for people."***

When you give it your all at work, you are putting a smile on God's face because he is pleased to see that He has entrusted the right person with such an important task. Treating every day like it matters and understanding that every day counts sounds great; however, it is not always easy.

Sometimes students may push every button that you have as if you were a controller for their game system. What should you do to prepare for those moments? What should you do in those moments?

Pray. Pray. Pray and then Pray Some More.

Every day we should spend personal time with God. As a follower of Christ, daily prayer is crucial because it allows us to communicate with God and speak to Him about any and everything.

When I make it a daily habit to pray in the morning and throughout the day while I am at work, I tend to have a better attitude.

Students may be challenging at times but there is nothing that a prayer for peace cannot remedy.

"You keep in perfect peace whose mind is stayed on you, because he trusts in you." Isaiah 26:3

I remember towards the end of the school year when my students became a bit antsy for summer and had to be given the same directions over and over; those days I prayed more than ever. One day, a student of mine kept getting up out of his seat, and I calmly told him to stop getting up and that if he did not listen, I would have to give him a consequence. I gave him several warnings that day, way more than usual. He asked me if I was alright and why I did not fuss at him; he told me, "Mrs. Young, you seem real chill and calm today." I laughed and continued my instruction.

I am willing to admit that I am far from perfect, and there have been days when I did not start my day off with prayer, and I know my students might have wished I had. On those days, my attitude was not very pleasant, nor was I as patient as my students needed me to be. I found myself easily annoyed, offended, and agitated on those days. Whether you are teaching in a public, private, Christian, or even home school setting, we cannot forget the importance of prayer. We have a direct line to God, and we can reach him any time of the day.

Isaiah 26:3 is loaded with so much truth. When I am in constant fellowship with God and my mind is on Him, then I will possess that unexplainable peace that He gives since I am trusting in Him. Every day has its problems, and you will need peace to face any situation that may arise. You will need peace to help you get through that observation. You will need peace to help you remain calm in a stressful situation, and you will need peace to help you execute that new lesson successfully. Whatever you need for that day, do not be afraid to talk to God about it. Do not be afraid to talk to Him throughout the day. If you keep your mind stayed on Him, He promises that you will be kept in perfect peace.

There may be days that you do not encounter any problems while you are working. Did you know you can still pray to God, even if nothing is going wrong and everything is going right? Even if your students are behaving like perfect angels, we should still pray, pray, and pray some more.

"I am willing to admit that I am far from perfect, and there have been days when I did not start my day

off with prayer, and I know my students might have wished I had."

God does not want to only hear from us when problems arise in our life. We can converse with God about anything; we can seek Him for guidance throughout the day. We may think our lesson is going to turn out amazing because we spent so much time in the planning phase, and we cannot think of any way for it to become even better. But what if you decide to pray before beginning your lesson and God instructs you to switch one little part, and you take heed to his voice, and it turns out better than expected. That is the way our God works. His thoughts are not like ours, and His ways are not like ours. We need to seek Him daily through prayer especially if we want to make each day count. I am convinced that prayer truly changes things and when you add faith to those prayers, you will be amazed at the possibilities.

Your Everyday affects the Long run

The task of a teacher is like that of an athlete that runs marathons. An athlete cannot expect to run half of the course and think their job is done. They must finish the race without giving out until they get across the finish line.

Likewise, a teacher must put in all their effort until the end of the school year. Every day a teacher comes to work, they are running a lap around that track and are one step closer to completing their marathon; they must keep up the momentum until they cross the finish line. The finish line would be the last day of school.

Your everyday actions show your true character. Students will always remember your character and work ethic, even if they forget the lessons you taught them. You want to make sure you maintain a good relationship with your students because you never know if God may somehow bring that student back into your life.

You want to be remembered as someone who was caring. It is okay to be strict, but there is a difference between being a disciplinarian and being borderline abusive by embarrassing your students. Attacking a person's character is not necessary. My pastor taught me the importance of talking to a person's action rather than their character. For instance, if you are upset someone fell through on a commitment to pick you up from the airport, when you speak to them, tell them how you feel about them not following through with the commitment. Maybe this led to you calling for an Uber or a taxi to pick you up when you were expecting them to be there. This might cause you to be upset but it is not effective, nor is it loving if you speak negative things about their character by calling them lazy and worthless.

This same approach must be taken with our students. If little Johnny is a student of yours who refuses to complete the assignment you have given and tries to get other students not to complete it either, he needs to be corrected for his behavior. You will need to explain to Johnny what rules he is breaking and speak to him about his action in refusing to follow the directions given. The consequences that follow are entirely up to you, but Johnny does not need to hear that he is lazy and a troublemaker.

Calling students stupid, lazy, or speaking negativity into their life by saying they will not amount to anything will not cause them to respect you. This approach is not effective; your students might fear you, but you will not have a long-lasting positive impact on them. You will be remembered as that teacher who was cruel and did not care about them.

A while back, I was at church when I saw a former student of mine, and it caught me by surprise. He remembered me and came over to hug me, and I introduced him to my husband. He shared with us his views on certain topics and explained to us how he was struggling with his faith. This former student of mine felt comfortable enough to share his thoughts and concerns with us, and I truly take it as an honor. We used this opportunity to encourage him in his faith, and at that moment, I realized my role as a teacher was so vital for this moment to take place. He listened to our advice and asked questions and it appeared that some of the weight he was carrying was being lifted off him. If I had treated this student poorly when he was my student and showed no love to him, this moment would not have been possible. God may not have been able to use me at this moment as His mouthpiece.

Remember that your students are still at an age where they are learning and growing; they are far from perfect, which I am sure is not a surprise to you. Think about it, what if they were your children? How you would want them to be treated and spoken to every day? Your students need love, direction, and dedication from their teacher EVERY DAY. It does not matter if they are 5, 10, 15, or even 18 years old, everyone should feel valued. They need you to reach beneath the surface and realize that you are impacting their lives, even if you cannot see how. You never know what the future may hold, so make each day count.

Prayer for the Day: Diligence

Dear Heavenly Father,

I would like to thank you for who you are and all the wonderful blessings you have bestowed upon me. I am grateful that I am in a position where I can teach my students not only important concepts and skills but also life lessons through my words and actions. Today, I ask you to help me to be a diligent worker, to constantly strive to be the best teacher I can be not only today, but every day I come to work. Help me to understand that every single student I have in my classroom is important to you, and they should be treated as such. Whether it be saying "Good Morning" every day, smiling as students enter, or making sure my lesson plans are in place, help me to be consistent in my behavior so that it becomes my character. Show me the importance every single day on why I should make every day count.

Amen.

Notes

"You have unique talents, gifts, and abilities that you bring to your classroom."

-Shanine Young

CHAPTER 3

BE THE BEST YOU THAT YOU CAN BE

Everyone else is already taken; your students, your colleagues, and especially the Lord needs you to be yourself. It is fine if you see areas you need to improve in, or you see qualities in someone that you admire, and you want to apply them to your life. The purpose of this chapter is not to criticize those who want to better themselves, but rather to shed light on the misconceptions that some teachers may have when it comes to their teaching and mannerisms. This chapter stresses the importance of knowing who you are and not allowing anything to cause you to be someone that you are not.

There will be times to accept and there will be times to reject.

Think back to your first year of teaching. Do you remember another teacher or administrator giving you advice on how to get respect from your students? Did they ever tell you not to smile during the first few weeks of school? Were you ever told that it is okay to embarrass a student if they become irate or behave unruly?

These are some of the worst advice ever! If you
desire to reach your students and show them you
are a teacher who cares about them, those would
not be the best measures for you to take. I enjoy
smiling, nine times out of ten if you see me
anywhere, you will catch me smiling.
Unfortunately, I followed this advice of no smiling
in front of your students, and I was not being true
to myself. After the first week of school, I realized
this no smiling business was not working for me.
There is nothing wrong with showing your
students you are a normal human being that smiles
at times. This popular advice that is filling the
minds of new teachers all around the world seems
to come from the belief that if you smile with your
students, during this critical time, they will see it
as a sign of weakness and will not respect you.
Smiling did not cause my students to treat me
disrespectfully; it is all about your classroom
management skills. Do you fail to stick to your
consequences? If you do, then smiling is the least
of your worries. Your students will view you as a
pushover or patsy if you do not do what you say
you are going to do. I learned a valuable lesson
during my first year of teaching; I realized that
there will be times when you will have to reject
some advice even if it comes from someone with
good intentions. You must be true to yourself; if
you are doing something just because it works for

someone else and it goes against your character, then you may need to take a step back and reevaluate what you are doing. Listen to advice from others but make up your mind that you are going to continue to be your genuine self to become the best you possible.

Do not allow anyone to stop you from shining!

You might have some hard-working teachers and administrators at your job, or you might have the exact opposite. It does not matter how others are behaving around you, you must decide that you are going to stay true to your value system and strive to be the best teacher that you can be. There may be teachers on your team or at your school whose work ethic is mediocre. They show up to work late almost every day, they miss deadlines all the time, they refuse to follow the rules and guidelines set in place by the administration or by the state, and they might even try to encourage you to be like them.

No matter what profession you are in, there will always be others who have different motivations as to why they do their job. I surveyed several educators all over the state of Florida, and over 50% of teachers stated their motivation for coming to work every day was the love they have for their students. Close to 30% of those surveyed stated that they showed up to work for the money, and 20% stated that the reason they show up every day is due to the fact they have colleagues who have become close friends. You will not always know the real reason as to why your coworkers perform their job the way they do, therefore you should not let your coworkers or anyone for that matter stop you from being the best you that you can be. You should never allow anyone to stop you from shining. If you want to change your classroom theme every year, do it! If you want to have mentoring sessions with your students during lunchtime, do it! If you want to reward your students consistently for their good behavior, do it! If you feel like giving Johnny a little more attention because he is acting out, do it! Do whatever you feel is best for your students. It can be difficult at times when it seems like the norm at your job is to slack off, but how about you set the bar high and Shine!

Identify the talents you bring to the table and develop them.

Are you an expert at lesson planning? Do you have superb organizational skills? Are you the teacher who creates the most engaging bell ringers?

Whether you know it or not, there are unique skills and talents inside of you waiting to be identified

and developed. Some of you reading this already know what they are. You know what you do best when you are in the classroom. If you are still trying to figure out some of your talents and skills, ask yourself what activities bring you the most joy in your classroom? What do you create or conduct with little to no effort that turns out amazing?

Some teachers have outstanding and effective classroom management skills and can always keep their class in order. Some teachers can easily grab the attention of others with little to no effort. Some teachers are very creative and can come up with activities on the spot for their students. Some teachers have the gift of listening and can empathize well with their students. No matter what you are bestowed with, you need to have the courage to accept yourself as you are and refrain from thinking you need to be like someone else. You have unique talents, gifts, and abilities that you bring to your classroom.

"You have unique talents, gifts, and abilities that you bring to your classroom."

How to identify what is within.

- **Ask God**: You can talk to God and ask Him to reveal to you the talents that He has blessed you with. He knows you better than you know yourself, after all He did create you. You would be surprised at what you can discover from spending some quiet time with Him.

- **Ask Yourself:** Sometimes you may need to search within to discover the talents or skills that you possess. Write down some of the things you are great at. Write down some of the things you enjoy doing. Write down some of the things you do well without much effort.

- **Ask a Close Friend or Trusted Colleague:** You might need to speak with a close friend and ask them for help in discovering some things you are good at. You can also try asking a trusted colleague to mentor or assist you in discovering areas that you should focus on and develop.

You might receive interesting responses and might even say, "How in the world does that relate to what I do in the classroom?" Do not lose hope, I am sure it can be applied. Sit down and think about ways to use that talent or skill of yours to help you become the best that you can be.

It took me a while to develop my talents and skills. I prayed, asked friends and colleagues at work, and I received similar responses. I was told I am very creative; I am musically inclined, and I can effectively motivate others. I figured I could use the first and third response and run with it. I focused on making my lessons more creative while encouraging and pushing my students more. I provided them with effective pep talks and feedback. I had no idea at the time that my musical skills could be used in the classroom effectively. I sat down one day and wrote down a plan. I decided I would use all the gifts, talents, and skills that I possess to become the best that I can be. I started making classroom jingles to help students learn and remember concepts and my students loved it. I even stepped it up a notch and recorded one of my jingles in my husband's music studio and played it for my students. We use music a lot in my class and I am glad I did not overlook this talent I was blessed with.

Whatever skills or abilities you are blessed with, use them, and do not let them go to waste. After you identify them, then it is time to create an action plan and decide how you will start to implement these skills and abilities. If you desire to reach your students and become the best version of yourself possible, you will have to continually strive for perfection and develop the qualities and skills that are pertinent to be an effective and innovative teacher.

Prayer for the Day: Confidence

Dear Heavenly Father,

I am so grateful to have a Father in Heaven who is concerned about me. I am so thankful to serve a God who knows everything about me. I know I am created for a purpose, and you have filled me with so many talents, gifts, and skills that can transform so many lives. There is only one "Me", and there is no one else in this world with my DNA. Help me Lord to walk confidently in how you made me and to never compare myself with others. Help me not to envy my coworkers. Help me strive to be excellent in everything I do, show me how to be more creative with my students. Help me to take pride in myself and come to work with the motive to reach and inspire my students to be the best they can be. While you are building my confidence, I pray you will allow my students to become more confident in their abilities as well.

Amen.

Notes

"I never did anything wrong in my entire life."

-No one

CHAPTER 4

MISTAKES ARE BLESSINGS IN DISGUISE

"I never did anything wrong in my entire life", said no one ever.

Everyone makes mistakes in life; being a teacher does not mean you are perfect. Sometimes students may view teachers with this mindset, they believe teachers are all-knowing and are shocked whenever their teacher slips up. Repeat after me, "I am a teacher and I make mistakes." The world did not end after you said that, life goes on. I remember a time when I use to beat myself up about making any little miscalculation or error; I was so hard on myself. After my second year of working in Education, I started to realize that it is perfectly normal to mess up sometimes. I gained so much insight and became more creative after analyzing my shortfalls. I am by no means saying it is okay to slack off at work and consistently underperform. We should take pride in what we do, seeking to be excellent in all things, but we must also understand that it is okay to fail every now and then.

I believe it is important for us as educators to practice what we preach. We tend to tell students that they should not be afraid of making mistakes. We make sure we leave room for error when it comes to our students. We have a plan B and differentiate our lessons to ensure that if a student is struggling to understand a concept, they will be able to try another approach. We find ways to accommodate and work with our students and encourage them when they mess up since they are still learning. But why don't we have this same approach with ourselves? Aren't we too still learning in this thing called life?

What can we do with our Mistakes?

- **Acknowledge them:** We must accept responsibility and acknowledge our mistakes. It is not a good idea to try to cover them up or ignore them because that may only make things worse.

Repeat after me, "I am a teacher and I make mistakes."

It requires a lot of humility to be able to admit when you did something wrong to anyone, much less to your students & colleagues, but it is worth it. Acknowledging your faults brings them to the light and lifts a weight off your shoulders. You will walk in true strength once you can admit your faults and be okay with them.

- **Forgive yourself of them:** There might have been instances when you ran out of time while teaching a lesson or you taught a concept completely wrong. It can be a bit stressful, especially if it causes you to get behind on your pacing guide for that quarter. That is just one of the many mistakes we can make as educators. Regina Moffett said it best "A faith-filled teacher takes risks and makes mistakes, knowing that ONE BAD lesson (or two) is not going to make God fall off the throne." We all know several different scenarios that could take place; however, we cannot allow our mistakes to consume us. Realize that the past is the past and you need to forgive yourself of whatever error you made. Remind yourself that you are doing the best that you can and refuse to allow your mistakes to make you miserable. Forgive yourself for your past and future mistakes because trust me, there are more to come.

- **Let it go and allow it to help you grow:** No matter what you did, it is time to let it go. You can no longer hold on to that mistake and allow it to make you miserable inside. We should not allow our mistakes to cripple us or affect us negatively, instead we should allow them to help us grow. We ought to look at them as if they are stepping stones. We can reflect on the choices we made and decide that we are going to do better next time. Even if we believe our faults were huge or unforgivable, we must understand that all events are blessings that we can learn from. We can use every circumstance and situation to help us become better people if we let go of negativity and walk with a positive mindset. I saw a post a year ago on Instagram that stated, "Everyone you meet has something to teach you." I will take it one step further and add that not only everyone but everything that comes your way has something to teach you. Trials, hardships, good times, and even mistakes can teach us valuable lessons if we allow them to and choose to learn something from them.

Maybe you forgot to turn in a document on time or you said some words to a student or colleague that you ended up regretting. You might have forgotten to send that important email or missed an important meeting. James 3:2 reminds us of how we all make many mistakes. Even if those choices led to some sort of discipline, the world did not end, and God did not fall off His throne. You can bounce back and bounce back strong from your mistakes; they are blessings in disguise, and it is time you start to realize it!

Prayer for the day: Perseverance

Lord, I come to you grateful for allowing me to see yet another day. I want to thank you for this opportunity to shape young minds. I know I am not perfect and that I make mistakes. I understand that you see everything and know everything that will happen before it happens, so Lord I ask that you help me to persevere through any future mistakes. Help me not to become weary in well doing. Galatians 6:9 states, "We will reap a harvest of blessings if we do not faint and give up." Help me to grow and learn from my mistakes. I pray that I will not allow them to cripple me but strengthen me. In all things I will give thanks, so even when I slip up, I will give you thanks because I know you are still watching out for me Lord. Remind me daily that your grace is enough, even in my weakness, I will keep pressing on.

Amen.

Notes

"The struggle you're in today is developing the strength you need for tomorrow."

-Unknown

CHAPTER 5

THE STRUGGLE IS REAL

Some people walk around with the misconception that teachers have it made since we get two months off in the summer. Some people believe teaching is such an easy career since some educators work with young people. Few individuals outside of the educational spectrum understand the daily internal and external struggles that teachers face.

Most educators work long hours, and then we end up taking a lot of our work home with us. We spend an excessive amount of time lesson planning, grading assignments and exams. Our job can be a very thankless one at times. Despite all that we do, we still deal with unwarranted criticism from peers, administration, parents, and society.

This chapter expresses some of the common struggles that teachers face and ways for us to successfully embrace and overcome these struggles.

The Struggle is Real in the Classroom

Our students come to us from all sorts of different backgrounds; they have different upbringings, morals, education, etc. As educators, we must differentiate not only our instruction but also our attention.

"If kids come to us from strong, healthy functioning families, it makes our job easier. If they do not come to us from strong, healthy, functioning families, it makes our job more important." -Barbara Colorose

All students are unique and so are their needs. Sometimes our students are dealing with so much dysfunction at home and they come to school to either release their stress or to find a haven. Our job is not always easy because there are times when we must go above and beyond to be there for our students in any way, shape, or form. If our students happen to come to us from dysfunctional homes, then what we do matters even more, and we should strive to reach them before teaching them.

Administration or other personnel may relay important information to us regarding our students or our students may end up confiding in us. We may become aware that one of our students is homeless or goes days without eating dinner at home. It is natural to be empathetic in these kinds of situations, but what happens to that empathy when this same student refuses to do work or disrespects you in front of the class? As teachers, unfortunately this is what comes with the job, we face many struggles in our classroom when it comes to the behavior and attitudes of our students. However, we are not called to be ordinary teachers who treat students kindly when they treat us kind, we ought to be a blessing to those who curse us or mistreat us, according to Luke 6:28-29. We know that hurt people essentially hurt people, so that is usually the case when our students are acting out and behaving unruly; they are dealing with hurt and are taking it out on the teachers and everyone else around them. The classroom is filled with many dilemmas from misbehavior, laziness, unpreparedness, and disrespect from students and the list goes on. It would take a whole memoir to discuss all the struggles we face in our class or learning center.

The Struggle is Real with Society

Teachers make more minute by minute decisions than brain surgeons, and that is why we go home so exhausted each day. Our brains are always working; lazy would be the last adjective to describe a teacher whose goal is to reach students while he/she teaches. Society might believe the lie that we are all lazy, but teachers are just like artists and entrepreneurs or anyone who is deeply committed to what they do. We never stop working, even when we are off the clock. On average, teachers spend 60-65 hours a week working during the school year so the two months off for summer break is well deserved in my opinion. I would be rich for all the times I have heard how lucky I am for having summers off, but what most people are unaware of is the fact that some of us do not just sit around doing nothing in the summer; we are still working. We are either planning for the next school year or holding down one or two summer jobs to ensure we are financially stable.

Society thinks our job cannot possibly be that hard but all the work and energy we put into our job can truly take a toll on us. Many educators deal with "teacher burn out" towards the middle or end of the school year from overexerting themselves. Some of us pile too many things on our plate or get burned out from all the learning and behavior problems we face in the classroom.

I remember a time when I was extremely overwhelmed with the overflow of assignments that needed grading. I had my mom and grandma to assist me with double-checking the multiple-choice answers on these assignments. I felt so drained during the week in question; my students were not performing as I thought they should have been, and the work just kept piling up. Not everyone knows the struggles we face on the regular and society tends to take our issues very lightly. They do not always consider the fact that we are still on the clock, even when we are off the clock, nor do they consider the fact that many educators work a second job throughout the school year. Some are striving to make ends meet and still going above and beyond to reach every student; if you fall into this classification, I tip my hat to you. You deserve a medal and hopefully, society will start to remove the veils from their eyes and begin to see what educators all around the world are facing.

The Struggle is Real with Administration

Some educators are blessed with amazing administrators or leaders that are extremely supportive and helpful, while some are stuck with overbearing micromanagers. Sometimes teachers are not treated like they are the professionals in their classrooms by administration. I have heard so many complaints about administrators telling teachers exactly how to do their job and monitoring their every move without allowing much input from the teacher. It would be helpful if they were providing constructive criticism and allowing open dialogue; some educators are afraid to be creative in their classrooms since they do not have much support from their administration. They feel they cannot do what they know is best for their students or openly share ideas with their administration.

This is a struggle for most teachers because they do not want to get written up for being incompliant, but they also do not want to ignore the needs of their students; this causes teachers to feel a bit helpless. There needs to be effective communication between teachers and administrators to ensure the students' needs are best met, and the teacher has enough autonomy to instruct his or her students.

Some of you might be struggling with feeling appreciated or valued by your administrators. You may feel like your voice is not being heard whenever issues arise. If a teacher has a disagreement with a student, and administration tends to take the side of the student before hearing the teacher's explanation, then that may cause a teacher to lose trust in their administration. I have dealt with a situation like this at one of my previous schools. I had an issue where a student would not follow the classroom expectations and I had to take the necessary steps and report this student. The situation escalated and the student did something out of the ordinary which called for serious attention. I was asked by my administration to explain what happened, and I felt as though my voice was not being heard. I was being blamed for what this student did even after explaining how I followed protocol. The administrator already knew what he/she felt should have happened in the situation and provided me with a non-realistic approach to handling this type of issue.

I could not possibly force a student to do something or to not do something. I could strongly encourage them, but I do not have the power to make them to do anything. At that moment, I felt as though if I had an administrator who was a little more understanding and could see things from my point of view, I would not have felt like I was not valued.

Keeping My Faith in the Struggle

If you are reading all of this and you are thinking, "What should we do when we face these struggles? How should we respond?" I want to encourage you to keep your faith during these struggles and difficulties. I had my share of difficult administrators and coworkers, but now I am blessed to have supportive administrators and coworkers who have become close friends over the years. I had to keep my faith in the struggle.

If you do not work at a Christian school or any other religious organization, it may be hard for you to juggle or maintain your faith and still be politically correct. I want to encourage you to keep your faith and hold tightly to it. As educators, we have so many things on our plate and it is so easy to get overwhelmed. Do not let the worries of the educational system bring you down. Do not let colleagues, administrators, students, or parents cause you to lose hope in the God you serve. All these struggles we face can either make us or break us. We must choose to remain hopeful, faithful, and resilient. "The struggle you're in today is developing the strength you need for tomorrow" is such a powerful and truthful quote that we should hold dear to our hearts. Everything you have faced or are facing as an educator is building you and refining you to become a stronger, better, and more equipped educator.

I deal with the challenges that are common in most inner-city schools. My school is classified as a low-income school; some of the students live in neighborhoods where there is so much violence and crime. These students need emotional support from their teachers. A lot of them do not always get the support they need at home, so I try my best to be as supportive and loving as I can be. I try to be their cheerleader, their disciplinarian, their nurturer, and of course their teacher. As teachers, it can be incredibly stressful wearing so many different hats, but our faith can help us stay afloat when we start to feel overwhelmed.

Due to this pandemic, educators all over the world are adjusting to a new normal; we are learning to adapt to distance learning just like our students. I saw a quote online that stated, "School closure does not mean extended spring break or early summer. Teachers and principals have never worked harder to make sure the kids get what they need." I wholeheartedly agree with this quote. This is a new challenge for teachers, but I have faith that we will continue to allow our struggles to refine us and grow us.

It is important to do whatever you need to do to remain sane and to keep your faith. Some may need to pray throughout the day, listen to a devotional on the way to work, or during planning time. Some may even need to listen to inspirational/gospel music during their lunch or planning. No problem is too big for the God we serve, and we must remember to remain steadfast and faithful even when we feel like giving up. As educators, we must embrace our struggles, whether it is with the administration, society, students, or parents. We must respond in love to our students, peers, administrators, and even the parents. The struggle is our greatest teacher and if we keep our faith in the struggle, we will come out as overcomers!

Powerful Encouraging Quotes for Educators

"Children are like wet cement, whatever falls on them makes an impression." - Haim Ginott

"Teaching is the one profession that creates all other professions."-Unknown

"Strength and growth come only through continuous effort and struggle."- Napoleon Hill

"Embrace struggle… It is your greatest teacher."

"I am not a teacher, but an awakener." – Robert Frost

"A teacher affects eternity; he can never tell where his influence stops." – Henry Adams

"Education is not the filling of a pail, but the lighting of a fire." –William Butler Yeats"

"You have unique gifts, talents and abilities that you bring to your classroom." -Shanine Alessia Young

"We're educators, we're born to make a difference." – Rita Piesson

Prayer for the Day: Overcoming

Dear Heavenly Father,

I am grateful for this profession; I am grateful for everything I have learned while working with these students of mine and while working with my colleagues. I know there are so many struggles and difficulties that I will deal with in this profession, but I am fully equipped to take on and overcome these challenges. I will face challenges with a smile because I know I will come out victorious. You are using me to impact so many lives, so I will continue to endure and push through even when it is difficult. When my students are pushing my buttons, or when my colleagues are upsetting me, I will be reminded of John 1:5 "The light shines in the darkness, and the darkness can never distinguish it." Therefore, I will shine brightly. I will gain control over any difficulty or problem that I face today and every day after that. I am an overcomer and a powerful educator!

Amen

Notes

Notes

Final Words

Thank you so much for taking the time out to read my book. I sincerely hope this encourages you, excites you and challenges you to transform and impact the lives of those around you. I would love to hear your thoughts and if anything written resonated with you. Feel free to email me at shaninealessia@gmail.com. I love educating and empowering people to live their best life and I think educators need to be educated and empowered as well. We pour so much of ourselves out, so it is important that we fill ourselves up.

To get a **FREE** Download of the Reaching While Teaching: Back to School Devotional for Teachers, head on over to my website. **www.shaninealessia.com**

If this book was a blessing or an encouragement to you, please share it with your friends and family and even your online friends by using the hashtag **#reachingwhileteaching.**

-Shanine Alessia Young